SPORTS SCIENCE PROJECTS
SC◯RE!

SLAM DUNK!

SCIENCE PROJECTS
with BASKETBALL

SPORTS SCIENCE PROJECTS

GOAL!
SCIENCE PROJECTS
with SOCCER

ISBN-13: 978-0-7660-3106-7
ISBN-10:   0-7660-3106-3

HOME RUN!
SCIENCE PROJECTS
with BASEBALL and SOFTBALL

ISBN-13: 978-0-7660-3365-8
ISBN-10:   0-7660-3365-1

SLAM DUNK!
SCIENCE PROJECTS
with BASKETBALL

ISBN-13: 978-0-7660-3366-5
ISBN-10:   0-7660-3366-X

WHEELS!
SCIENCE PROJECTS
with BICYCLES, SKATEBOARDS and SKATES

ISBN-13: 978-0-7660-3107-4
ISBN-10:   0-7660-3107-1

SPORTS SCIENCE PROJECTS

SCORE!

SLAM DUNK!

SCIENCE PROJECTS
with BASKETBALL

Robert Gardner
and
Dennis Shortelle

Enslow Publishers, Inc.
40 Industrial Road
Box 398
Berkeley Heights, NJ 07922
USA

http://www.enslow.com

Library of Congress Cataloging-in-Publication Data

Gardner, Robert, 1929–
    Slam dunk! science projects with basketball / Robert Gardner and Dennis Shortelle.
        p. cm. — (Score! sports science projects)
    Includes bibliographical references and index.
    Summary: "Presents several science experiments and science project ideas using physics and basketball"—Provided by publisher.
    ISBN-13: 978-0-7660-3366-5
    ISBN-10: 0-7660-3366-X
    1. Physics—Experiments—Juvenile literature. 2. Science—Experiments—Juvenile literature. 3. Basketball—Juvenile literature. 4. Science projects—Juvenile literature. I. Shortelle, Dennis. II. Title.
    QC25.G374 2010
    530—dc22   2008024879

Printed in the United States of America

052010 Lake Book Manufacturing, Inc., Melrose Park, IL

10 9 8 7 6 5 4 3

To Our Readers: We have done our best to make sure all Internet Addresses in this book were active and appropriate when we went to press. However, the author and the publisher have no control over and assume no liability for the material available on those Internet sites or on other Web sites they may link to. Any comments or suggestions can be sent by e-mail to comments@enslow.com or to the address on the back cover.

♻ Enslow Publishers, Inc., is committed to printing our books on recycled paper. The paper in every book contains 10% to 30% post-consumer waste (PCW). The cover board on the outside of each book contains 100% PCW. Our goal is to do our part to help young people and the environment too!

Photo Credits: © Kenneth Eward/Photo Researchers, Inc., p. 40; Shutterstock, pp. 6, 80.

Illustration Credits: © 2008 by Stephen Rountree (www.rountreegraphics.com)

Cover Illustration: Shutterstock

CONTENTS

Indicates experiments that are followed by Science Project Ideas.

INTRODUCTION

Do you like to shoot hoops with your friends? Maybe you enjoy watching your favorite basketball team on television or at school. With this book, you can not only enjoy basketball, but also do some science experiments. You will learn more about the sport, its history, and its players, as well as something about science.

Most of the experiments can be done with a basketball on a basketball court. For some experiments, you will need someone to help you. It would be best if you work with a person who enjoys experimenting and basketball as much as you do.

If any risk of injury is involved in an experiment, it will be made known to you. In some cases, to avoid any danger, you will be asked to work with an adult. Please do so. We don't want you to take any chances that could cause an injury.

Some experiments involve action on the court. Before exercising, it is a good idea to stretch your muscles and warm up. Professional athletes warm up before their games. Your school coaches or gym teachers can suggest some routines. Or you can check sports books in the library.

Like a good scientist, you will find it useful to have a notebook. Use it to record ideas, notes, data, and any conclusions you draw from your experiments. By doing so, you can keep track of the information you gather and the conclusions you reach.

Science Fairs

Some of the experiments in this book contain ideas you might use as a science fair project. Those experiments are indicated by a symbol ⬤. However, judges at science fairs do not reward projects or experiments that are simply copied from a book. A model of a basketball court would not impress most judges. However, finding the terminal velocity of a falling basketball would attract their attention.

Science fair judges tend to reward creative thought and imagination. It is difficult to be creative or imaginative unless you are really interested in your project. Therefore, try to choose an investigation that appeals to you. And before you jump into a project, consider, too, your own talents and the cost of the materials you will need.

If you decide to use an experiment or idea found in this book for a science fair, find ways to modify or extend it. This should not be difficult. As you experiment, you will discover that new ideas come to mind. Such ideas could make excellent science fair projects, particularly because the ideas are your own and are interesting to you.

If you decide to enter a science fair and have never done so, you should read some of the books listed in the Further Reading section. These books deal specifically with science fairs. They provide helpful hints and useful information that will enable you to avoid the pitfalls that sometimes trouble first-time entrants. You'll learn how to prepare appealing reports that include charts and graphs, how to set up and display your work, how to present your project, and how to relate to judges and visitors.

The Scientific Method

Scientists look at the world and try to understand how things work. They make careful observations and conduct research. Different areas of science use different approaches. Depending on the problem, one method is likely to be better than another. Designing a new medicine for heart disease, studying the spread of an invasive plant such as purple loosestrife, and finding evidence of water on Mars require different methods.

Despite the differences, all scientists use a similar general approach in doing experiments. It is called the scientific method. In most experiments, some or all of the following steps are used: observation of a problem, formulation of a question, making a hypothesis (a likely answer to the question), making a prediction (an if-then statement), designing and conducting an experiment, analyzing results, drawing conclusions, and accepting or rejecting the hypothesis. Scientists then share their findings by writing articles that are published.

You might wonder how to start an experiment. When you observe something, you may become curious and ask a question. Your question, which could arise from an earlier experiment or from reading, may be answered by a well-designed investigation. Once you have a question, you can make a hypothesis. Your hypothesis is a possible answer to the question. Once you have a hypothesis, it is time to design an experiment to test the consequences of your hypothesis.

Suppose your question is "Does the height to which a basketball bounces depend on the height from which it is dropped?" Your hypothesis might be that the bounce height depends on the height from which the ball is dropped. In the experiment, you would drop the ball from different heights and measure the height to which the ball bounces.

During the experiment, you would collect data. You would measure the drop height and bounce height for a number of different drop heights Then you would draw conclusions.

Two terms are often used in scientific experiments— *dependent variables* and *independent variables*. The dependent variable here is the bounce height. Drop height is the independent variable. It doesn't depend on anything. After the data is collected, it is analyzed to see if it supports or rejects the hypothesis. The results of one experiment may lead you to a related question, or they may send you off in a different direction. Whatever the results, something can be learned from every experiment.

Safety First

Most of the projects included in this book are perfectly safe. However, the following safety rules are well worth reading before you start any project.

- Never experiment with flames or electrical appliances without adult supervision.

- Do any experiments or projects, whether from this book or of your own design, under the supervision of a science teacher, coach, or other knowledgeable adult.

- Read all instructions carefully before proceeding with an experiment. If you have questions, check with your supervisor before going any further.

- Maintain a serious attitude while conducting experiments. Fooling around can be dangerous to you and to others.

- Wear approved safety goggles when you are doing anything that might cause injury to your eyes.

- Have a first aid kit nearby while you are experimenting.

- The liquid in some thermometers is mercury (a dense liquid metal). It is dangerous to touch mercury or breathe mercury vapor, and such thermometers have been banned in many states. When doing these experiments, use only non-mercury thermometers, such as digital thermometers or those filled with alcohol. If you have a mercury thermometer in your home, **ask an adult** if it can be taken to a local thermometer exchange location.

IT'S ALL ABOUT THE BALL

One of the nice things about basketball is the price to play. Once you have a basketball and a pair of sneakers, you have everything you need to play the game. Public basketball courts, either outdoors or indoors, are fairly common. Other sports, such as hockey and football, require costly equipment. Furthermore, you can practice shooting baskets by yourself. You don't need anyone else to have fun.

In this chapter, you will examine and measure the ball used to play the game of basketball. You will measure its "bounciness," the energy changes involved when it bounces, and how much it is compressed during a bounce.

EXPERIMENT **1.1**

How Big Is the Ball?

MATERIALS
- basketball
- thin string
- felt-tip pen
- meterstick or yardstick
- a partner
- 2 straight sticks
- ruler
- platform balance that can weigh to the nearest gram or tenth of an ounce or better (electronic balance in science lab, mail scale, fish scale, kitchen scale)

A basketball is about the size of a globe you might find in a social studies classroom. But exactly how big is a basketball? To find out, you can measure its circumference (distance around the ball).

1 Wrap a thin string around the middle (equator) of a basketball. Use a felt-tip pen to mark the points where the string meets (see Figure 1a).

2 Use a meterstick or yardstick to measure the distance between the two points. What is the circumference of the basketball in centimeters or inches? If you measured the circumference in centimeters, what is the circumference in inches? You need to know that

$$1 \text{ inch} = 2.54 \text{ cm}$$

If you measured the circumference in inches, what is the circumference in centimeters?

3 Figure 1b shows you how to measure the diameter (distance across the center) of a basketball. Have a partner hold two sticks straight up and down (vertically) on opposite sides of the basketball. Use a ruler to measure the distance between the vertical sticks. What is the diameter of the basketball in centimeters? In inches?

According to the rules, a men's basketball should have a circumference of between 29 ½ and 30 inches (74.9–76.2 cm). This means its diameter should be between 9 ¹³/₃₂ and 9 ⁹/₁₆ inches (23.9–24.3 cm).

The circumference of a women's basketball should be 28 ½ to 29 inches (72.4–73.7 cm), with a diameter of 9 ¹/₁₆ to 9 ¼ inches (23.0–23.5 cm).

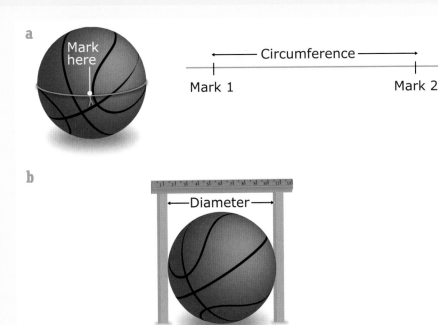

a

Mark here

Circumference

Mark 1   Mark 2

b

Diameter

FIGURE 1.
a) Use a string to measure the ball's circumference.
b) Use two vertical sticks and a ruler to measure the ball's diameter.

How closely do your measurements agree with the basketball rule book?

4 What is the ratio of the ball's circumference to its diameter (circumference ÷ diameter)? Is this number similar to any number you have heard of in your math classes?

5 Find the weight of your basketball. Put it on a platform balance that can weigh in grams or ounces. What is the ball's weight in grams? In ounces? In kilograms? In pounds? You need to know that

1 kilogram weight (kg)* = 2.2 pound (lb)
1 pound = 16 ounces (oz)
1 ounce = 28.4 grams (g)
1,000 g = 1.0 kg

According to the rules, a men's basketball should weigh between 20 and 22 ounces (1.25 and 1.38 pounds) or 0.57–0.63 kg or 570–630 g.

A women's basketball should weigh 18 to 20 ounces (1.13 to 1.25 pounds) or 0.51–0.57 kg or 510–570 g.

Does your basketball's weight meet the rules?

SCIENCE PROJECT IDEA

Measure the circumference and diameter of a number of different balls—baseball, tennis, soccer, Ping-Pong, etc. For each ball, find the ratio of the circumference to the diameter. What do you conclude?

* A kilogram is a mass, not a weight (force). By writing "kilogram weight," we mean the weight of a kilogram, which is 9.8 newtons (N). Scientists use the metric system, which is compared with U.S. customary units in Table 1.

Mass and Weight

People are often confused about the difference between mass and weight. To understand the difference, pretend you take a trip to the Moon. Before the trip, you sit on one pan of a giant equal-arm balance. To balance your mass (the amount of matter in your body), 50 kilograms are placed on the other pan. So your mass is 50 kg.

Table 1. **METRIC AND U.S. CUSTOMARY UNITS OF MEASUREMENT**

Length	
Metric	**Equivalent U.S. Customary**
1 meter (m)	1.09 yards, 3.28 feet, 39.37 inches
1 centimeter (cm) 0.01 m	0.3937 inch
1 millimeter (mm) 0.001 m	0.03937 inch
Volume	
Metric	**Equivalent U.S. Customary**
1 liter (L)	1.057 quart
1 milliliter (mL) 0.001 L	0.001057 quart
Mass	
Metric	**Equivalent U.S. Customary**
1 kilogram (kg)	0.0685 slug
1 gram (g) 0.001 kg	0.0000685 slug
Weight (Force)	
Metric	**Equivalent U.S. Customary**
1 newton (N)	0.224 pound

Your weight is the force with which Earth pulls you toward its center. We call that force gravity, and it can be measured in pounds. If your mass is 50 kg, your weight is 110 pounds. This weight can be determined by having you hang from a large spring scale or by standing on a bathroom scale.

When you reach the Moon, a giant equal-arm balance will show that your mass is still 50 kg. There is still the same amount of you. Your weight, however, as measured on a spring or bathroom scale, is only 18 pounds.

Your weight on the Moon is only one-sixth as much as it is on Earth. Why?

The force of gravity on the Moon is about one-sixth as large as it is on Earth. However, your mass, as measured on an equal-arm balance, remains the same. Both sides of the balance—you on one side, standard masses on the other—are pulled toward the Moon with the same force. But the amount you stretch a spring is far less because the Moon's pull on you is only one-sixth as much as Earth's.

In other words, mass is the amount of matter in something. Weight is the force that gravity exerts on that matter. Way out in space, far from any stars or planets, your weight might be zero, but your mass would remain the same.

After winning the gold medal in 2000 at the Olympic games in Sydney, Australia, the United States basketball team could do no better than bronze at the 2004 games in Athens, Greece. As a result, U.S. basketball officials decided to develop a true national team rather than putting a group of all-stars on the court. They asked NBA players to join the team for at least three years. Joining the team would involve attending regular practices and exhibition games, and playing in the Olympics. The "Redeem Team," selected to revive American basketball success, was led by captains LeBron James, Kobe Bryant, and Dwyane Wade.

The 2008 Beijing Olympics offered these American players a chance to win the gold again. Spain, the world champion team, was the final hurdle on the path to restoring United States Olympic superiority in basketball. Although Spain played well, Team USA captured the gold medal with a 118–107 victory.

EXPERIMENT **1.2**

Weighing Air Using a Basketball

MATERIALS

- basketball
- platform balance that can weigh to the nearest gram or tenth of an ounce or better (electronic balance in science lab, mail scale, fish scale, kitchen scale)
- air pump with valve for inflating balls
- pen or pencil
- notebook

It is not easy to weigh air or any gas. However, a basketball can be used to show that air does have weight.

1 Insert a valve used to inflate a basketball. If you hold the valve near your face, you can feel the air coming out of the ball.

2 Let the air out of the ball. There will still be some air in the ball, but it will be at the pressure of the air outside the ball.

3 Place the ball on a platform balance. Very carefully weigh it to the nearest gram or tenth of an ounce. Record its weight.

4 Use an air pump to fill the ball with air until the ball is very hard.

5 Place the inflated ball back on the balance. Again, weigh it to the nearest gram or tenth of an ounce. Record its weight. Does air have weight? How can you tell?

Basketball is the only sport ever created by just one person. It was invented in 1891 by James Naismith, a physical education teacher at the YMCA Training School in Springfield, Massachusetts (now called Springfield College). He was looking for a sport that could be played indoors.

Since most sports involve a ball, Naismith settled on a soccer ball. He decided that players could advance the ball only by passing it. (Dribbling did not become part of the game until about 1896.) Since a ground-level goal, like hockey, might lead to the roughness and injuries Naismith wanted to avoid, he asked for boxes. The janitor could only find peach baskets. Naismith nailed the peach baskets to the lowest level of the gymnasium balcony. The height was ten feet, and it remains the regulation height of baskets today. A pole was used to get the ball out of the basket after each goal. After about a year, wire mesh baskets replaced the peach baskets. Backboards were introduced in about 1895 to keep balcony fans away from the ball and to protect the baskets from spectator interference.

The first game, an intramural game within Naismith's class, was probably played in early December, 1891. The teams played fifteen-minute halves. The final score was 3–0. The game was an immediate hit, and word of the new pastime spread rapidly. YMCAs and colleges were the earliest groups to sponsor teams.

SCIENCE PROJECT IDEA

Under adult supervision, do an experiment to find the weight of air at ordinary air pressure. How can you find the density of the air in your experiment?

EXPERIMENT **1.3**

A Bouncing Basketball

> **MATERIALS**
> - basketball
> - hard floor or basketball court
> - tape
> - 2 yardsticks and a clothespin, or a wall to which you can apply tape
> - a partner
> - notebook
> - Table 2
> - graph paper
> - ruler
> - pencil or pen
> - Figure 2b
> - different surfaces such as wood, concrete, tile, linoleum, macadam, carpets, grass, dirt

The rules of basketball are specific about the "bounciness" of the ball. A men's basketball dropped from a height of six feet (as measured from the bottom of the ball) should rebound to a height of between 49 and 54 inches (as measured from the top of the ball). For a women's basketball, it must rebound to a height of between 51 and 56 inches.

It may seem strange that both measurements are not from the bottom of the ball. However, it makes it easy for an official. After dropping the ball, he or she just has to hold his or her hand at the minimum required bounce height. If the ball hits the official's hand, it meets the rule.

1 Test a basketball to see whether it meets the rule. Tape two yardsticks together, or put a strip of tape on a wall six feet above the floor. (If you have access to a basketball court, strips of tape at these heights may be in place.) Drop the ball from a height of six feet onto a basketball court. Have a partner watch to see what height the top of the ball reaches after bouncing. Drop the ball several times to be sure you have the correct bounce height. If you use two yardsticks, a clothespin could be used to mark the proper bounce height, as shown in Figure 2a.

2 Repeat the experiment. This time be more scientific. Measure both drop height and bounce height from the bottom of the ball. What is the ratio of bounce height to drop height? For example, if the bottom of the ball bounces to a height of 44 inches, the ratio is:

$$\frac{44 \text{ in}}{72 \text{ in}} = 0.61$$

Record that information in a data table like the one in Table 2.

3 What is the ratio of bounce height to drop height when the ball is dropped from heights of five feet, four feet, three feet, and two feet? Remember to repeat each experiment several times to ensure a correct measurement. Record all your data in your notebook.

4 Plot a graph of bounce height versus drop height. Plot bounce height on the vertical axis. Plot the corresponding drop height on the horizontal axis.

The authors' results for this experiment are shown on the graph in Figure 2b. Because the points lie very close to a straight line, the authors drew a straight line through the points. They decided the best average ratio was

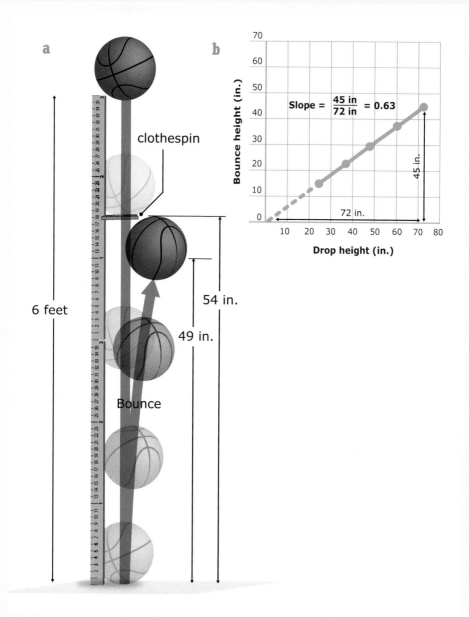

a

b

clothespin

6 feet

54 in.

49 in.

Bounce

Bounce height (in.)

Slope = $\dfrac{45\ in}{72\ in}$ = 0.63

45 in.

72 in.

Drop height (in.)

FIGURE 2.
a) Testing a basketball for "bounciness" according to the rules
b) A graph of the authors' data for Experiment 1.3

Table 2. BASKETBALL BOUNCES FROM DIFFERENT DROP HEIGHTS (MEASURING BOTH DROP HEIGHT AND BOUNCE HEIGHT FROM THE BOTTOM OF THE BALL)

Height from which ball is dropped (inches)	Height to which ball bounces (inches)	Ratio: bounce height ÷ drop height
72		
60		
48		
36		
24		

the slope of the graph, which is 0.63 (see calculation in Figure 2b).

How do the authors' results compare with yours?

5 Use your graph to predict the bounce height of the basketball when it is dropped from heights of 30, 42, 54, and 66 inches. How good were your predictions?

6 How does the surface on which the ball is dropped affect its bounce? To find out, try dropping the ball on different surfaces, such as wood, concrete, tile, linoleum, as well as macadam, carpets, grass, and dirt. How can you explain differences in bounce height on different surfaces?

SCIENCE PROJECT IDEAS

- Basketballs are generally inflated to a gauge pressure of 7 to 9 pounds per square inch. How does air pressure affect the bounce height of a basketball? Can you find a mathematical relationship between a basketball's bounce height and its gauge pressure?

- Compare the bounciness of a basketball with other sports balls. You might try balls used in baseball, tennis, golf, Ping-Pong, soccer, lacrosse, and squash. You might extend your investigation by including two extremes—a Super Ball and a clay ball. How can you explain the differences in bounciness?

- How does temperature affect the bounciness of different sports balls?

- What is an elastic collision? An inelastic collision? Do basketballs have elastic or inelastic collisions with the floor? How about a clay ball?

EXPERIMENT **1.4**

How Many Bounces?

MATERIALS
- basketball
- 2 yardsticks
- a partner
- calculator (optional)

1 Let a basketball bounce from a height of five feet (60 inches) as measured from the bottom of the ball.

2 Have a partner watch the bottom of the ball as it bounces upward. Have him or her measure the height to which the ball bounces, as measured from the bottom of the ball.

3 Repeat the experiment several times to measure the bounce height as accurately as possible.

4 To what fraction of its original height did it bounce? For example, if it bounced to a height of 45 inches, the fraction is

$$\frac{45}{60} = \frac{3}{4} \text{, or } 0.75.$$

5 Next, release the ball from the height to which it bounced. If it was 45 inches, release it from 45 inches.

6 To what height does it bounce this time? Again, repeat the experiment several times to measure the bounce height as accurately as possible.

7 To what fraction of its original height did it bounce? How does this fraction compare with the first one? Are they very nearly the same?

8 Based on what you have found, predict how many bounces the ball will make if released from a height of five feet.

9 Drop the ball from a height of five feet. Let the ball continue to bounce until it stops. How many times did it bounce? How good was your prediction?

Why Does a Ball Bounce?

Drop a basketball onto a hard surface and it bounces. Drop a clay ball onto the same surface and it does not bounce. Why does one bounce and not the other?

A basketball held above the floor has potential (stored) energy. Its potential energy is the energy you gave it when you lifted it to a height above the floor. If you lifted it twice as high, it would have twice as much potential energy. Earth's gravity pulls it downward. That gravitational force will make the ball accelerate. As the ball falls, its potential energy changes to kinetic (motion) energy. When it hits the floor, the ball quickly comes to a momentary stop, again storing some of the kinetic energy as potential energy. Just as quickly, it turns potential energy back into its kinetic energy as it bounces upward. But it does not have all the kinetic energy it had before the bounce (see Figure 3). As a result, it rises to only a fraction of its original height—it no longer has all its potential energy. Since energy is conserved (never lost), where did that energy go?

The answer lies in friction. There is friction between the ball and the floor during the bounce, and there is friction within the ball itself. Friction produces thermal energy (heat). Some of the ball's kinetic energy is transformed (changed) into heat. If you add the heat generated and the kinetic energy remaining after the bounce, the sum will equal the original potential energy.

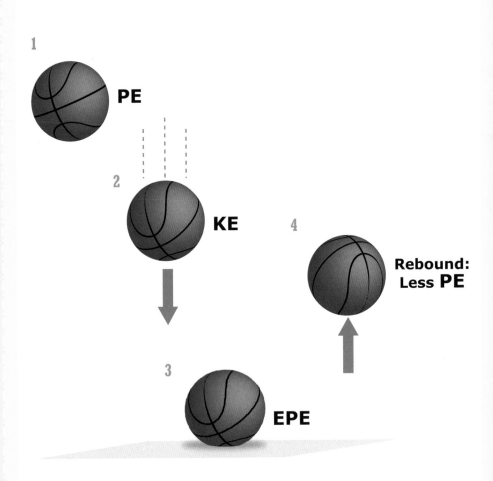

FIGURE 3.
(1) Ball has potential energy (PE).
(2) Falling ball has kinetic energy (KE).
(3) Compressed ball has elastic potential energy (EPE).
(4) After rebound, ball has less KE because it doesn't bounce as high, and will acquire less PE.

When a clay ball falls to the floor, all its kinetic energy is converted to heat.

What happens as a basketball reaches the floor? The bottom of the ball is compressed like a spring with coils that have been squeezed together. Some of its kinetic energy changes to heat, but much of it is changed to elastic potential energy (EPE). Energy is stored as elastic potential energy in a compressed spring. Similarly, elastic energy is stored in the compressed ball.

As the ball returns to its original shape, the EPE changes back to kinetic energy. As a result, the ball bounces upward. As the ball continues to bounce, the process will be repeated several times. In the end, all the potential energy the ball had when it was first dropped will be changed to heat.

SCIENCE PROJECT IDEAS

• Look up the meaning of *coefficient of restitution*. Then measure the coefficient of restitution of a basketball.

• Measure the coefficient of restitution of other balls used in sports. Which one bounces highest?

• What is the coefficient of restitution of a Super Ball?

EXPERIMENT **1.5**

How Much Is a Basketball Compressed During a Bounce?

MATERIALS

- fine white flour, talcum powder, or chalk dust
- smooth surface
- basketball
- yardstick
- tape measure
- large piece of wrapping paper
- pencil
- drawing compass
- two 7-ounce Styrofoam cups
- dry sand
- laboratory thermometer: use only non-mercury thermometers, such as those filled with alcohol or digital thermometers
- scissors

To see how much a basketball is compressed when it hits the floor, you can do an experiment.

1 Spread some fine white flour, talcum powder, or chalk dust on a smooth surface.

2 Hold a basketball three feet above the white powder. Let the ball fall without any spin onto the powder. Catch the ball before it bounces again.

3 Look carefully at the part of the ball that hit the floor. You should be able to see a faint circle of powder. Using a tape measure, determine the diameter of the circle.

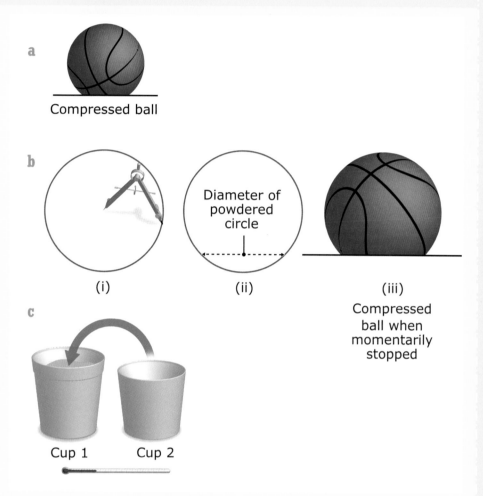

FIGURE 4.

a) A basketball is compressed when it is momentarily stopped at the low point of its bounce.

bi) Use a compass to draw a circle that has the diameter of the basketball: 9.5 inches.

bii) Connect points on the circle that are separated by the diameter of the powdered circle.

biii) You have drawn the compressed ball when it was momentarily stopped.

c) Convert kinetic energy to heat by making sand fall quickly between two insulated cups.

How much of the ball (what area) hit the floor? Remember, the area of a circle is πr^2, where r is the radius ($\frac{1}{2}$ the diameter).

In order to make a significant powdered circle on the ball, the ball must have been compressed and its surface deformed (see Figure 4a). The ball had its maximum elastic potential energy when it was compressed the most.

The ultimate individual scoring record in basketball is 100 points in a single game. At the college level it had been done twice, but no one believed that scoring one hundred points in a professional game was realistic because of the size, skill, and experience of pro players.

On March 2, 1962, Wilt Chamberlain and the Philadelphia Warriors were playing the New York Knicks. On this night, Chamberlain scored 23 points in the first quarter, and had 41 by halftime. At the end of the third quarter he had 69 points. By the fourth quarter, the fans were yelling "shoot" every time "The Stilt" had the ball.

The Warriors began in-bounding the ball to Chamberlain. The ball was in his hands most of the time. He stopped playing defense and stayed on the offensive side of the court. With just over one minute left in the game, Wilt dunked his ninety-eighth point. With 46 seconds remaining, Chamberlain scored his one hundredth point of the game. The Warriors won 169–147.

4 Find a large piece of wrapping paper. Use a drawing compass to draw a circle that has the same diameter as the basketball—about 9.5 inches (see Figure 4bi). Draw a straight line across the circle that is the length of the diameter of the powdered circle. Place the endpoints of the line on the larger circle (Figure 4bii). Extend the straight line (Figure 4biii). You have made a drawing of the ball at maximum compression on a surface—when the ball was momentarily stopped before bouncing upward.

5 Repeat the experiment, but this time drop the ball from a height of six feet. Do you think the diameter of the powdered circle will be twice as large? How about the area?

6 To see that kinetic energy can be converted to heat, half fill a 7-ounce Styrofoam cup with dry sand. Measure the temperature of the sand.

7 Cut the top rim off a second Styrofoam cup. Push the second cup upside down into the first one (Figure 4c). You can now turn the cups over without spilling sand.

8 Turn the cups over so that sand falls from one cup into the other. Turn the cups again so that sand falls back into the first cup. Quickly turn the cups back and forth 200 times.

9 Measure the temperature of the sand again. What evidence do you have that kinetic energy can be converted to heat?

SCIENCE PROJECT IDEAS

- How does the air pressure in the ball affect the amount the ball is compressed when it bounces?

- Compare the amount that other sports balls are compressed during a bounce.

- Design and do an experiment to show that repeated bouncing of a ball can produce heat.

- Hang a spring or a strong rubber band from a hook. Attach a weight to the spring or rubber band. Let the weight fall and watch the motion. How is it like a bouncing ball? How is it different?

GALILEO, NEWTON, AND BASKETBALL

Galileo (1564–1642) and Newton (1642–1727) lived long before basketball was invented. However, their work provides us with an understanding of what happens on a basketball court. The scientific laws they developed were the result of their experiments. These laws of science can help you play the game better.

You will do experiments similar to those done by Galileo 400 years ago. You will also test Newton's laws of motion. Scientific laws like Newton's are not decided by a legislature. They are rules about nature discovered through observation

37

and experimentation. These laws are statements for which there are no known exceptions. However, if exceptions are found, scientific laws can be changed. Sometimes new observations or experiments cause scientists to modify the laws. So far, there have been no exceptions to Newton's laws of motion.

EXPERIMENT 2.1

Galileo and Basketball

> **MATERIALS**
> - basketball
> - tennis ball
> - Figure 5
> - 2 nickels
> - table

Galileo Galilei, commonly known by his first name, was a great scientist. He did many experiments. In one experiment he showed that objects, both heavy and light, fall at the same rate. You can do a similar experiment.

1 Hold a basketball and a tennis ball side by side. The bottom of each ball should be the same distance above the floor. Release both balls at the same time. As you can see, they fall side by side. Both hit the floor at the same time.

   Galileo showed that falling objects accelerate (speed up) as they fall. He found that the speed of a falling object is proportional to the time it has been falling. If a ball is falling at a speed of 1.0 m/s after 0.1 s, its speed will be 2.0 m/s after 0.2 s. This is more difficult to prove. Figure 5 shows how an object accelerates as it falls.

   Galileo made another discovery. When one ball is launched horizontally, and a second identical ball is released at the same time and falls vertically, both fall with the same acceleration.

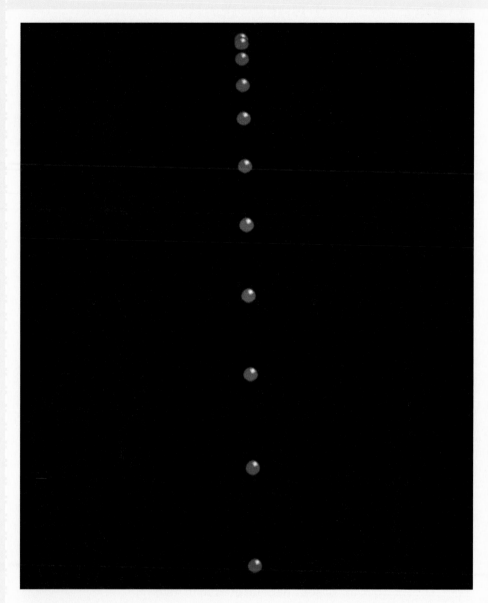

FIGURE 5.

In flash photography, the camera's shutter is kept open. A bright light flashes periodically. In these flash photos, the light flashed every $\frac{1}{10}$ second. You can see that for every $\frac{1}{10}$ second, the ball falls faster. The ball is accelerating.

FIGURE 6.

A 10-cent experiment can show that an object moving horizontally falls at the same rate as one that falls straight down.

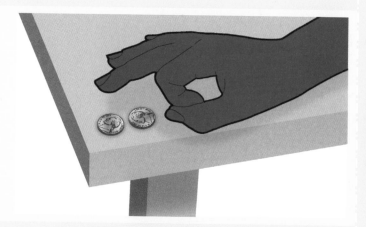

You can do a similar experiment. It too will show that an object with a horizontal velocity* falls downward at the same rate as one falling straight down.

2 Place a nickel at the edge of a table. Place a second nickel a short distance behind the first one, as shown in Figure 6. Snap your finger against the second nickel so that it strikes the first one. The first nickel will fly off horizontally and land some distance from the table. The second will fall almost vertically to the floor. Listen carefully! Do the coins strike the floor at the same or at different times? What can you conclude about the downward acceleration of the coins?

---

* The word *velocity* has a different meaning than *speed*. A velocity has both speed and direction. A person running north at 5 meters per second (m/s) has a velocity of 5 m/s north. If you know only someone's speed, you do not know which way he or she is moving. If you are given the person's velocity, you know the direction he or she is moving as well as the speed.

SCIENCE PROJECT IDEAS

- Using Figure 5, determine the downward acceleration of the billiard ball. Then do an experiment of your own to measure the acceleration of a falling object.

- Why do flat sheets of paper and Styrofoam balls fall more slowly than basketballs?

The most famous early women's basketball team was the All-American Red Heads based in Caraway, Arkansas. The Red Heads played by men's rules. They competed against local male teams as they traveled from town to town. The Red Heads were paid a part of the admission fees. The team sometimes played seven or eight games a week. They won 70 to 80 percent of their games during their 50-year reign from 1936 to 1986.

The Red Heads traveled to every state and played in Mexico, Canada, and the Philippines. The team traveled 20,000 miles during each season, which ran from October to May. At first they traveled in station wagons. Later, they rode in limousines.

There were team rules. First, the team members had to be redheads, natural, dyed, or wigged. Second, they had to serve as role models for young women. Smoking in public was forbidden. Makeup was considered part of their uniform. To avoid cliques, they were required to switch roommates and change seats in the limos.

In 1999, the All-American Red Heads was inducted into the Women's Basketball Hall of Fame in Knoxville, Tennessee.

EXPERIMENT 2.2

Newton and Basketball

MATERIALS

- basketball
- basketball court
- Figure 7
- chalk or flour
- level sidewalk or path
- water
- water balloons
- bicycle
- bicycle helmet
- a partner
- medicine ball
- skateboard
- bathroom scale

Sir Isaac Newton was an English physicist and mathematician regarded by many as the greatest scientist who ever lived. His first law of motion is based on Galileo's laws of motion. Galileo observed that, barring friction, an object in motion will stay in motion, without any additional push. He also observed inertia—the property of a moving body to stay in motion, or a stationary object to stay at rest. Newton's first law states that an object maintains its state of motion unless acted upon by a force (a push or a pull). It has two parts: (1) An object at rest will remain at rest unless a force acts on it. For example, suppose a basketball is at rest on the court. It will stay there until someone picks it up or pushes it (puts a force on it). (2) If an object is moving, it will continue to move at the same speed and in the same direction unless a force acts on it.

1 Place a basketball on the court. It doesn't move. Now give it a push. Notice how it rolls along at almost the same speed for a long time. Eventually, it will stop rolling because a force (friction) acts on it. You will examine that force in another experiment.

2 Walk along the court at a steady speed carrying a basketball. Let the ball drop off the tip of your fingers (Figure 7). Continue to walk at the same speed. Notice that the ball continues to move with you. It had your forward speed. It continues to have your speed. What happens if you stop walking after you release the ball? Does the ball continue to move forward?

3 Here's another experiment to illustrate Newton's first law of motion. Use some chalk or flour to make a target on a level sidewalk or path.

4 Fill a few water balloons. Seal them by tying off the necks.

5 Be sure the path is clear. Put on your bicycle helmet. Hold a water balloon against your bike's handlebar and ride toward the target. When the balloon is directly above the target, release it. Did the water balloon hit the target? If not, where did it land? Why do you think it did not hit the target?

6 Repeat the experiment while riding your bike at different speeds. How does the speed at which your bike is traveling change the horizontal distance the balloon travels before it hits the ground?

7 Repeat the experiment. This time release the water balloon at a point that you think will make it hit the target. How close did you come?

FIGURE 7.
Why does a ball you drop while walking continue to move along with you?

Newton's second law of motion involves the forces that change motion. It states that if you apply a net force to an object, the object will accelerate in the direction of the force. (Net force equals the force applied less any opposing force.) It also states that the acceleration depends on the mass of the object. Suppose the same force acts on a basketball and a bowling ball. The acceleration of the basketball will be larger than the acceleration of the bowling ball. This is not surprising. It is harder to move a bowling ball (which has more mass) than a basketball. We say the bowling ball has more inertia.

8 Hold a basketball with both hands. Make several two-handed bounce passes to a partner. At first, push the ball very gently. Gradually increase the force with which you push the ball. What happens to the speed of the pass as you increase the force?

As you can see, the ball accelerates as you push it. It starts at rest and leaves your hands with some speed. The harder you push, the greater the ball's acceleration. As a result, when you apply more force to the ball, it gains more speed.

Newton's third law of motion states that for every action there is an equal and opposite reaction. What this means is that if you push on the floor, the floor pushes back on you with an equal force. When you push on a basketball, the ball pushes back on you with an equal force. But since you have much more mass than a basketball, your acceleration is very small. This is especially true if you are wearing basketball sneakers. The friction between your shoes and the court keeps you firmly attached to the floor, which is attached to the building, which is attached to Earth (a large mass, indeed).

9 Try passing a medicine ball (or other heavy object) while sitting on a skateboard. Do you and the ball accelerate in opposite directions?

10 Stand on a bathroom scale while holding a medicine ball. What happens to your weight on the scale when you throw the ball upward?

11 What happens to your weight if you suddenly lower your body by bending your knees? Can you explain why it happens?

SCIENCE PROJECT IDEAS

• Use a level air hockey game to illustrate Galileo's law of inertia (Newton's first law of motion).

• Place two skateboards on a smooth, level surface. Have two people sit on the boards. Have one person push the other. What happens? What happens if one person is much heavier than the other?

• Measure the height, in meters, through which the water balloon in Experiment 2.2 fell. The time for it to fall is approximately the square root of two-tenths the height (h). That is,

$$\text{time to fall} = \sqrt{0.2h}$$

Use this information, together with other measurements you can make, to find the speed of your bike when you drop a water balloon.

EXPERIMENT **2.3**

Acceleration and Circular Motion

MATERIALS
- **adult driver**
- helium balloon on a string
- car

Does a turning car, Earth, or anything moving along a circular path have an inward or outward acceleration? That is, does it accelerate toward or away from the center of the arc in which it is moving? You can find out by doing an experiment.

1 Obtain a helium balloon attached to a string. Move the balloon at a steady speed. Then make it accelerate. You will see it move in the direction it is accelerating.

   The helium balloon can serve as an accelerometer. It moves in the direction in which it is accelerating.

2 Take the balloon with you on an automobile trip. Hold the balloon inside the car, and keep the windows closed.

3 While an adult is driving the car, watch the helium balloon on its string. What happens to the balloon when the car accelerates forward? What happens to the balloon when the car accelerates in a negative direction (brakes or slows down)?

4 Watch carefully when the car goes around a curve. Which way does the balloon move? What is the direction of the car's acceleration?

When the NBA was formed in 1949, all its players were white. An unspoken agreement among owners excluded African-American players. The owners reasoned that if blacks joined the league, white fans would lose interest. Ned Irish, owner of the New York Knicks, finally broke the unsaid agreement. Irish wanted to sign Nat "Sweetwater" Clifton, who was playing professionally with the Harlem Globetrotters, an African-American basketball sensation. The other owners voted no. Six months later, the owners backed down when Irish threatened to pull his team out of the league if he couldn't sign Clifton. This paved the way for black players in the NBA. In 1950, three African Americans—Clifton, Earl Lloyd, and Chuck Cooper—joined the NBA.

Long after his retirement, former Boston Celtic Chuck Cooper admitted being the "first" was hard. He was often not allowed to stay at the team hotel because of his color. Once in Raleigh, North Carolina, Cooper played a game, then boarded a train back to Boston rather than stay in a separate hotel. Future Hall of Famer Bob Cousy, a white player, was so upset by the discrimination that he rode the train back to Boston with Cooper.

EXPERIMENT **2.4**

Basketball and Friction

MATERIALS

- leather-soled shoe, or another type of shoe, newspaper, and tape
- basketball court
- weight, such as a paperweight, doorstop, or large smooth stone
- tape
- shoestring
- spring scale from a school science department or a scale from which small fish are hung for weighing
- basketball shoe or sneaker

A rolling ball eventually comes to rest because a force acts against its motion. That force is friction. Friction always acts against motion. An experiment will show that basketball shoes are made to provide lots of friction.

1 Place a leather-soled shoe on a basketball court. (If you can't find such a shoe, tape some newspaper to the bottom of any other kind of shoe.) Put a paperweight, doorstop, or a large smooth stone in the shoe. The added weight will prevent it from sliding too easily.

2 Using tape, attach one end of a shoestring to the toe of the shoe, as shown in Figure 8. Tie the other end of the string to a spring scale.

3 Keeping the spring scale close to the floor, pull the shoe slowly across the floor. Look at the scale as it moves. How much force is needed to move the shoe along the floor?

Shoe   Spring balance

FIGURE 8.
How large is the frictional force between the shoe and the floor?

According to Newton's third law, the force needed to move the shoe at a slow speed is equal to the frictional force opposing the motion.

4 Repeat the experiment, but this time put the weight in a basketball shoe. What force is needed to move the basketball shoe slowly along the floor? How does the frictional force on the basketball shoe compare with the force on the leather-soled shoe?

Why do you think friction between shoes and the floor is important in basketball?

SCIENCE PROJECT IDEA

Design an experiment to compare friction when wearing basketball shoes with friction when wearing socks.

In an interview with *Sports Illustrated* during his rookie year, a young Michael Jordan said he would "like to play in at least one All-Star game." This was a modest goal for a man many believe to be the best basketball player to ever step onto a court.

But Jordan's life in basketball was not always a success. As a high school sophomore he did not make the basketball team. By the next year, he had grown four inches. In his senior year, he was a high school All-American and received a scholarship to the University of North Carolina. After three years on their team and selection as the national College Player of the Year, Jordan turned pro. He was the third player chosen in the 1984 NBA draft, picked by the Chicago Bulls. This was an Olympic year, and as College Player of the Year Jordan was an easy choice for the team that won a gold medal in Los Angeles. Jordan's second Olympic gold medal came in 1992 when he was a member of the Dream Team in Barcelona, Spain.

"Air Jordan" was a five-time MVP, a six-time NBA champion, and a fourteen-time All-Star. He retired in 2003 with the NBA's highest career scoring average of 30.1 points per game. He is still part of the game as a part owner of the NBA's Charlotte Bobcats. An ESPN poll to determine the greatest athlete of the twentieth century ranked Jordan above Babe Ruth and Muhammad Ali.

EXPERIMENT **2.5**

Basketball and More about Friction

MATERIALS
- basketball
- basketball court

Friction between the ball and the floor, backboard, and rim is important in basketball.

1 To see how a basketball normally bounces, make a bounce pass onto a smooth floor with as little spin as possible. Notice that the ball bounces up from the floor at about the same angle it hits the floor (see Figure 9a).

2 Make the same pass but give the ball lots of topspin (see Figure 9b). How does the bounce of a ball with topspin compare with the bounce it took when there was no spin?

There is friction between the spinning ball and the floor. This friction prevents the ball from sliding along the floor. Figure 9b shows how the frictional force makes the ball with topspin bounce differently. It gives the ball more horizontal speed.

3 Next, make a bounce pass, but give the ball backspin (see Figure 9c). How does this ball's bounce compare with the others? Explain why the ball bounced the way it did.

Can you make the ball bounce straight up when you pass it forward? Can you make it bounce back toward you?

4 Using what you have learned, can you make the ball spin so that it bounces to the right or left of its original direction?

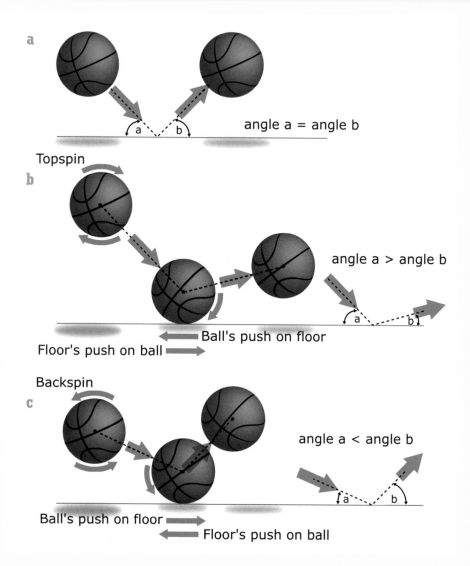

angle a = angle b

Topspin

angle a > angle b

Ball's push on floor

Floor's push on ball

Backspin

angle a < angle b

Ball's push on floor

Floor's push on ball

FIGURE 9.

a) A ball without spin bounces up at about the same angle that it hits the floor.

b) With topspin, friction between the ball and the floor creates a force that propels the ball forward.

c) With backspin, friction between the ball and the floor creates a force that pushes the ball backward as it bounces up.

SCIENCE PROJECT IDEAS

- Do experiments to see how the spin on a Ping-Pong ball can affect the ball's motion and make it follow different paths.

- Applying backspin to a basketball when making a shot increases the likelihood of making a basket. Use what you know about spinning balls, friction, and Newton's laws of motion to explain why.

- In earlier times, basketball players often made underhand foul shots with two hands. They started the shot with the ball between their knees and released it about head high with a lot of backspin. Try making foul shots this way. Does it improve your foul shooting percentage?

In 1979, the NBA faced financial difficulties. Fan interest was fading and attendance was low. Fortunately for the league, two players—Larry Bird and Earvin "Magic" Johnson—renewed fan enthusiasm. During the 1980s, these two men led their teams to seven NBA championships, earning six MVP trophies for their individual talents.

The rivalry between the two stars began in 1979 when Magic Johnson led Michigan State to the national college title, beating Bird and the Indiana State Sycamores. The rivalry continued for a decade in the NBA. In 1984, the exciting championship series between the Lakers and the Celtics came down to Game Seven. Before a record TV audience, Larry Bird scored 27 points to give the Celtics their fifteenth NBA crown. The following season, in a rematch of the same teams, Johnson's Lakers won the championship in six games.

In 1992, the first time professionals could play in the Olympics, both men played on the United States Olympic "Dream Team." Led by Bird and Johnson, the team stormed through the tournament and won the gold medal. Both Bird and Johnson are in the Basketball Hall of Fame.

EXPERIMENT 2.6

Impulse, Momentum, and "Soft Hands"

MATERIALS

- basketball
- basketball court
- a partner
- water balloons

To pass or shoot a basketball, you have to apply a force to the ball for a period of time. The force you apply multiplied by the time you apply it is called impulse:

$$\text{impulse} = \text{force} \times \text{time} = F \times t$$

Once the impulse is over, the ball has momentum. Its momentum is equal to its mass times its velocity.

$$\text{momentum} = \text{mass} \times \text{velocity} = m \times v$$

To see how the size of the impulse affects a basketball's momentum, you can do an experiment.

1 Using one hand, hold a basketball at nearly arm's length in front of your chest. Using your other hand, push the ball forward for a short time (Figure 10a). You gave the ball a small impulse.

2 Hold the basketball close to your chest. Using your other hand, push the ball forward with the same strength as before (Figure 10b). This time you pushed for a longer time. Therefore, the impulse was greater. Is the momentum the ball acquires also larger? How can you tell?

3 Next, throw the ball as you would a baseball, but with the same force as you used in steps 1 and 2 (see Figure 10c).

FIGURE 10.
Compare the results when you apply an impulse (F x t) to a basketball using the same force for a) a short time; b) a longer time; c) a still longer time.

This time you apply the force for an even longer time. How does the bigger impulse affect the ball's momentum after it leaves your hand?

You can reduce an object's momentum by applying an impulse against the momentum. You do this every time you catch a ball. You can apply the impulse in different ways. You can apply a large force for a short time, or you can apply a smaller force for a longer time.

4 Have a partner pass a basketball to you. Try to catch the ball without moving your hands very much. You will apply a relatively large force for a short time.

5 Again, have the partner pass the basketball to you in a similar way. This time let your hands move with the ball. You applied a small force for a longer time to remove the ball's momentum.

Players with "soft hands" let their hands move with the ball when they catch it. The impulse they use to catch the ball involves a small force over a relatively long time.

6 Try catching water balloons using soft hands. What happens if you use "hard hands?" Would you dare to catch eggs with "soft hands?"

In the early days of baseball, players did not wear gloves. They quickly learned to catch the ball over as long a time as possible. Even so, many fingers and hands were broken before the baseball glove was invented.

The Paralympics are the Olympic games for persons with a disability. They are usually held in the same city that hosts the Olympic Games. The idea for these types of games started in 1948 when Sir Ludwig Guttmann started a sports competition in England for World War II veterans with spinal cord injuries. The first official Paralympics were held in 1976 at the winter games in Sweden.

There are twenty Paralympics sports, including wheelchair basketball. In 2008, the U.S. women's team beat Germany to win the gold medal. Australia won the gold medal for the men's team.

SCIENCE CAN MAKE YOUR SHOTS COUNT

In this chapter you will see how science can improve your shooting. You will find there is a "best place" on the backboard for layup shots. You will investigate the illusion of the floating layup and how it is related to your center of mass. You will find the best angle for launching your long shots. It may not, as you will find, be the best angle for making the longest pass. And you will see how distance from the basket affects your shooting percentage.

EXPERIMENT **3.1**

Making Layup Shots

MATERIALS
- basketball
- basketball court
- pen or pencil
- notebook
- calculator

For most players, layups are their best shot. However, if you are playing a good defensive team, it may be too hard to get close enough to the basket for a layup.

The important thing to remember in making a layup shot is what you learned in Experiment 2.2. A basketball that you are carrying or dribbling has the same velocity that you do. When you make a layup, you are usually moving quickly toward the basket. So is the basketball. If you push the ball forward as you shoot, it will probably probably bounce hard against the backboard and miss the basket. Try to *place* the ball on the backboard in the region L or R (shown in Figure 11) as you make your layup. Place the ball in region L if your layup is from the left side of the basket. Place it in region R if it is from the right side. The ball has velocity because it is moving with you. It will continue to have that velocity when it hits the backboard.

A good layup shooter has to be able to use either hand. Your defender will try to stay between you and the basket. Therefore, try to shoot layups from the right side with your right hand and from the left side with your left hand. That way your shooting hand is farther from the defender. It will be less likely that he or she will be able to block your shot.

FIGURE 11.

Layup shots are most likely to go through the hoop if placed in zone L or R. R is for right-hand shots from the right side. L is for left-hand shots from the left side.

1 Start about 15 feet from the basket on the right side of the court. Dribble quickly to the basket and make a layup with your right hand. Try to place the ball on region R, as shown in Figure 11.

2 Repeat this right-hand layup shot 10 times. How many layups did you make? How many did you miss? What was your shooting percentage? Record this data in your notebook.

3 Repeat the experiment for left-hand layups. Try to place the ball onto region L.

4 Repeat the layup shots from both sides of the court, but try to place the ball at the center of the backboard. What was your shooting percentage this time? Record the data in your notebook. What can you conclude?

The WNBA is the nation's professional basketball league for women. In 1996, interest in women's basketball was rising after Team USA won the gold medal at the Atlanta Olympics. At that time, women who wanted to continue their basketball careers beyond college had to play in Europe, Asia, or Australia. The time was right for a new women's league in the United States, and the NBA wanted to be in on it.

The NBA owners were looking for ways to make better use of their arenas during the off-season and an opportunity to market the game to new customers. The eight new women's teams were partnered with NBA clubs, and the team names were similar to those of the men's teams. In order not to conflict with the NBA and college seasons, the WNBA games were played in the summer. There were also some rule differences. The women used a smaller ball, and the three-point arc was closer to the basket. Attendance at games was beyond expectations. By its second season, the WNBA was attracting foreign players to what had become the world's top women's league.

By 2008, the league had grown to 16 teams. League rules had become more like those of the NBA, attendance was growing, and the league gained some independence. The 2008 Olympic team that won the gold medal in Beijing was made up of star WNBA players.

EXPERIMENT **3.2**

Center of Mass

MATERIALS
- yardstick
- padded sawhorse or the soft arm of a sofa
- a wall
- full-length mirror

An object's center of mass (COM) is the point where all its mass can be considered to be located. It is the object's balance point—the point at which forces causing it to rotate are balanced.

The COM of some objects is easily located. For example, the COM of a basketball is at its center. The COM of a yardstick is at the 18-inch mark.

1 Put your finger under the 18-inch mark on a yardstick. Does the stick balance? What happens if you put your finger under the 20-inch mark?

Your body has a COM. It is probably located a few inches below your navel.

2 To find your COM, lie rigidly on a padded sawhorse or the soft arm of a sofa (see Figure 12). When your body is balanced, your center of mass will be directly above the fulcrum. Try it! What is the approximate location of your center of mass?

3 What happens if your COM is not above your body's points of support (your feet)? To find out, stand with your right leg and shoulder firmly against a wall. What happens when you lift your left foot?

FIGURE 12.
To find your center of mass, balance yourself on a soft, sturdy support.

4 Stand with your heels and shoulders against a wall. Try to touch your hands to your toes. What happens?

5 Stand with your toes touching a wall. Try to stand up on your toes. What happens?

6 Your body automatically adjusts to keep your COM above a point of support. To see how, stand in front of a full-length mirror. Lift your left foot. How does your body adjust to keep your COM above your right foot? What happens if you lift your right foot instead of your left?

SCIENCE PROJECT IDEA

Design and do experiments to find the COM of different objects.

EXPERIMENT 3.3

Center of Mass: A Model

MATERIALS

- level surface
- tall block (or tape 2 short blocks together)
- short block same width as tall block
- protractor

You can make a model to show why it is important to keep your center of mass (COM) above and inside your points of support (your feet).

1 Place a tall block like the one in Figure 13a on a level surface. It represents a player who is standing straight up. Where is its COM?

2 Slowly tip the block. Use a protractor, as shown, to measure the tip angle. At what angle does it tip over (fall)? At what angle is its COM beyond a point of support?

3 Place a block with the same width but about half as tall (see Figure 13b) on a level surface. It represents a player who has his legs bent to stay low. Where is its center of mass (COM)?

4 Slowly tip this shorter block. Use the protractor to measure its tip angle. At what angle does it tip over (fall)? At what angle is its COM beyond a point of support?

Why should you keep your body low and your feet apart when guarding an opponent?

Why should you keep your body low and your feet apart when faking an opponent before driving to the basket?

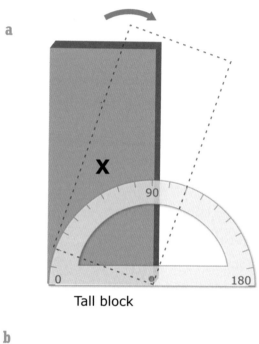

a

X

90

0   180

Tall block

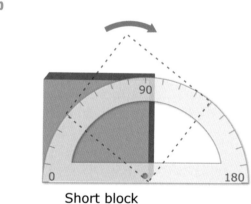

b

90

0   180

Short block

FIGURE 13.

The x marks the vertical block's center of mass. a) Through what angle must this tall block be tipped before its center of mass is beyond a point of support? b) Through what angle must this shorter block be tipped before its center of mass is beyond a point of support?

EXPERIMENT 3.4

Center of Mass and the "Floating" Layup

MATERIALS

• Figure 14

Some professional and college basketball players can appear to float or hang in the air as they make a long-leaping layup.

1 Examine the graph in Figure 14. It shows the increased height of a player's COM during a floating layup. It also shows the horizontal and vertical distances traveled at 0.1-second intervals after leaving the floor. In making the graph, it was assumed that the player was moving horizontally at 22.8 ft/s (15.5 mph). It was also assumed that the player leaped with an upward velocity of 12.6 ft/s (8.6 mph). (Remember, as seen in Figure 6, vertical and horizontal velocities are independent of one another.) Finally, it was assumed that his COM was 3 feet above the floor.

IGURE 14.

graph showing
ιe path of a
layer's center
f mass during a
oating layup.

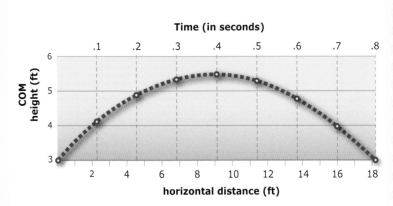

2 Why might this player appear to "float"? Hint: How long does it take for the player's COM to reach half of its maximum vertical height of 5.5 feet?

3 How long is the player in the upper half of his leap? How long is the player in the lower half of his leap?

4 What percentage of the time in the air is spent in the upper half of the leap? What percentage of the time in the air is spent in the lower half of the leap?

SCIENCE PROJECT IDEA

Take a video of a player making a floating layup. Analyze the time spent in the upper and lower halves of the layup.

Yao Ming is China's gift to basketball. As captain of the Chinese national team, the 7-foot 6-inch center was the flag bearer at the opening ceremonies of the 2008 Beijing Olympics. Even as a child, great things were expected of him. Ming's parents were both basketball players and very tall compared to the average Chinese citizen. His mother, at 6 feet, 2 inches, played for the women's national team. His father was a 6-foot, 7-inch shooter for the Shanghai Sharks in China's best basketball league.

Despite his family background and size, Yao Ming was more interested in reading and military history as a child. At age twelve, Chinese sports leaders pushed the young giant to Shanghai's sports school. As he continued to grow, he climbed the Chinese basketball ladder. In 1997–98, the seventeen-year-old joined his father's old team, the Sharks. In three seasons he turned an average team into league champs. His success moved him up to the national team when he was eighteen. In 2002, the Houston Rockets made Yao Ming the first pick from an international basketball league.

As a pro, Yao Ming was an immediate success—good, but not yet great. In his meeting against Shaquille O'Neal and the champion Lakers, Ming did well, scoring six quick points and blocking O'Neal's first three shots. His play led to his selection to the 2006 All-Star team, starting ahead of O'Neal. By 2008, China's most popular player was averaging 18 points per game in the NBA.

EXPERIMENT **3.5**

The Best Angle for Making Set Shots

MATERIALS
- basketball court
- basketball
- a partner
- Figure 15a
- notebook
- pen or pencil

Young players can more easily launch the ball using the set shot than the jump shot. In a set shot, the legs and body provide some of the force needed to project the ball. The jump shot depends on a force provided by only the arm and wrist.

1 Stand at a point on the court where you feel confident of making your set shot.

2 Try launching your shots at different angles. Try everything from line drives to rainbows (see Figure 15a). If you use the one-hand set shot, remember to keep your elbow under the ball. Let the ball go off the tips of all five fingers with a snap of the wrist to give the ball backspin.

3 Have a partner estimate the upward angle at which you launch your shots. Figure 15a gives a rough idea of launching angles. Make as many shots as possible. Have your partner keep a record of the shots and the launch angles.

Which launch angle results in more baskets made? What is your best shooting angle? Is it closer to a rainbow or a line drive?

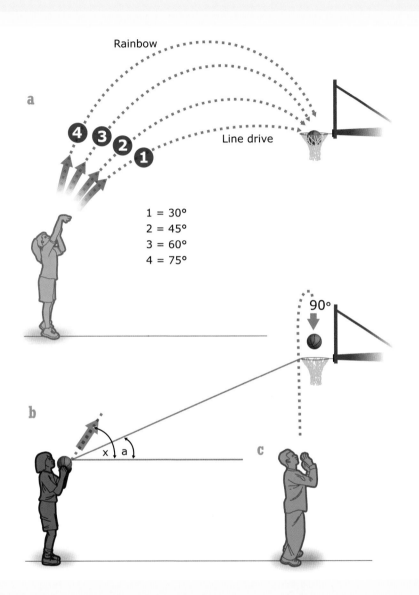

Rainbow

a

Line drive

1 = 30°
2 = 45°
3 = 60°
4 = 75°

90°

b

x a

c

FIGURE 15.

a) Try launching shots at different angles.

b) Angle a is the angle of incline from a player's hands to the rim of the basket. Angle x is 45° + $\frac{1}{2}$ angle a. Angle x is the best angle to launch a shot.

c) At 90°, you have to stand under the basket to make the shot.

One scientist (Peter Brancazio) believes that the best shooting angle is 45 degrees plus half the angle of incline to the basket (see Figure 15b). Suppose a shot is taken 20 feet from the basket. According to Brancazio, a shot made from five feet above the floor should be launched at 52 degrees. Such a shot is much closer to a rainbow than a line drive. A player seven feet tall might actually launch jump shots at an incline of 0 degrees (even with the basket's rim). Such a shot should then be made at 45 degrees.

Of course, a ball approaching the basket from an angle of 90° would never miss (Figure 15c). However, the shot would have to made from under the basket.

EXPERIMENT **3.6**

Shooting Percentage and Distance

MATERIALS

- basketball
- basketball court
- measuring tape or yardstick
- a partner
- notebook
- pen or pencil
- pocket calculator (optional)

How does distance from the basket affect your shooting percentage? To find out, calculate the percentage of shots you can make from various points on the court. Choose points similar to those shown by the Xs in Figure 16.

1 Use a measuring tape or yardstick to measure the distance from directly under the basket to the point from which you will shoot.

2 Ask a partner to rebound or retrieve your shots and pass the ball back to you.

3 Take 10 shots from each shooting position. Record the distance and the number of baskets made per 10 shots. Try shooting from different locations with the same distance (such as opposite sides of the key). Then vary your distance from the basket as well. If you become tired, rest before trying more shots.

4 For each distance on the court from which you took shots, add all the shots taken. Then add all the baskets made. To determine your shooting percentage, divide the baskets

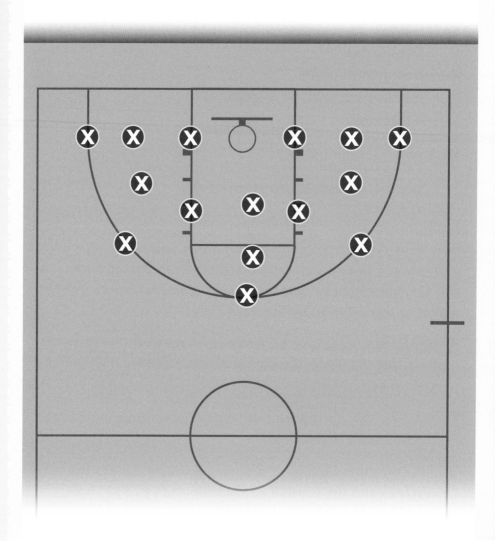

FIGURE 16.

How does distance from the basket affect your shooting percentage?
Try shooting from the places marked with Xs.

made by the number of shots taken. Multiply that decimal fraction by 100 to change it to a percentage. For example, suppose you took a total of 50 shots from five locations 20 feet from the basket. If you made 27 baskets, your shooting percentage would be:

$$\frac{27}{50} = 0.54 \times 100 = 54\%$$

Make a chart of your results like the one in Table 3 (where one example is shown).

Table 3. SHOOTING PERCENTAGES FROM VARIOUS DISTANCES.

Distance (ft)	Shots taken	Baskets made	Decimal fraction of baskets/shots	Percentage of shots made
20	50	27	0.54	54

How does distance affect your shooting percentage? Is there some distance on the court from which your shooting percentage is better than anywhere else? Is there some place on the court where your shooting percentage is better than anywhere else? How can knowing this spot help you to improve your game?

Measure your foul shooting percentage. Is it your best shooting percentage?

THE PASSING GAME

Basketball players spend a lot of time practicing their shots. This makes good sense. However, passing is also a vital part of the game. No player can consistently dribble through an opposing defense. Consequently, this chapter is about the science of the passing part of the game. You will investigate the best angle for throwing the very long pass and why such a pass can be dangerous. You will also see how drawing arrows (vectors) can help you make successful passes.

The United States had won every gold medal since basketball became an Olympic sport in 1936. But in 1972 the Soviet Union (now Russia) threatened U.S. dominance. The United States and Soviet teams met for the gold-medal game. With time running out, U.S. player Doug Collins stole a pass and drove to the basket. He was fouled. Collins sank his first free throw. While shooting his second, a buzzer sounded. Collins calmly sank the shot. It put the Americans ahead by one point.

With three second left, the Russians missed a long shot. The U.S. team celebrated, but the Soviets claimed they had called a time out between Collins's free throws, which the referee had ignored. The General Secretary of the International Basketball Federation came down from the stands. He ruled in the Soviets' favor. The Soviets got the ball. Their next shot missed. Again, they protested, claiming the referees started play before the clock was reset. Three seconds were added and play began once more.

The Russian center grabbed a long pass and placed it in for the win. The country that invented basketball lost the gold medal 51–50.

The United States filed a protest. It was rejected. The team refused to attend the medal ceremony or accept their silver medals. Thirty years later, Olympic officials asked the team to reconsider. The team again refused the medals. At least two team members have wills stating that even after their deaths, their families cannot accept the medals.

EXPERIMENT **4.1**

The Best Passing Angle for Maximum Distance

MATERIALS

- sheet of cardboard about 18 inches square
- protractor
- yardstick
- pen or pencil
- water pistol
- water
- day without wind, or garage or basement
- a partner
- small stones
- water hose with a nozzle that allows you to make a fast, narrow stream

Suppose you want to throw a basketball as far as possible. You want the ball to reach a teammate at the other end of the court. At what angle should you launch it?

Except for bounce passes, most passes in basketball are launched at an angle above the horizon. Otherwise, gravity may make the ball fall short of its intended mark.

1 From a sheet of cardboard, make a large half-protractor. To do this, simply extend the lines of an ordinary protractor (see Figure 17a).

2 Use a water pistol to shoot water at different angles. Do this outdoors on a day when there is no wind. Or, with permission, do it inside in a garage or an unfinished basement. Have a partner use a small stone to mark the farthest point that the water lands (see Figure 17b).

Be sure that the water gun is always the same distance above the floor. The gun's barrel should be parallel to an angle line of the large protractor. In Figure 17b, the barrel is at 20 degrees.

At what angle does the water travel farthest?

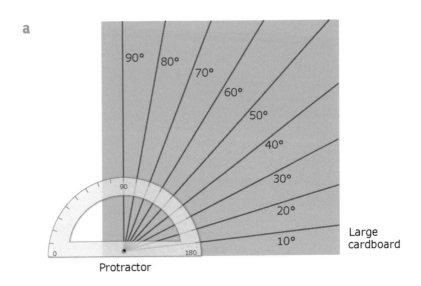

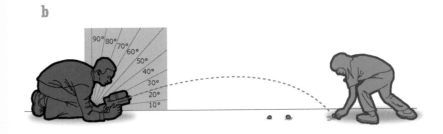

FIGURE 17.

a) Make a large half-protractor.
b) Shoot the water gun at different angles. Mark each distance the water travels with a small stone.

3 How far does a shot launched at 60 degrees travel? How far does a shot launched at 30 degrees travel? Why do you think they both travel about the same distance horizontally? Which shot (30 or 60 degrees) has the greater horizontal (sideways) velocity? Which shot has the greater vertical (upward) velocity?

4 In warm weather, you can repeat this experiment with a water hose. Use a nozzle that allows you to make a narrow stream. Does the greatest range occur at the same angle as it did with the water gun? At what angle should you throw a basketball to make the longest pass possible?

SCIENCE PROJECT IDEA

A baseball outfielder should throw home on a path like a line drive rather than like a fly ball. Use a stopwatch to show that this is true. Then explain why it is true.

As a junior, Kobe Bryant was the Pennsylvania high school player of the year. As a senior, he led Lower Merion High School to a 31–3 record and a state championship. *USA Today* selected him as National Player of the Year. At seventeen, Bryant turned pro. The youngest player to make the move joined the Lakers in 1996. For the first two years, Bryant was the Lakers sixth man (the first player off the bench). By 2000, the Lakers were the best team in the NBA. They began a three-year title run led by Shaquille O'Neal and Bryant. As the young Laker star improved and adjusted to the pro style of play, awards followed. He became a ten-time NBA All Star and an eight-time member of the All Defensive team. He was twice voted MVP of the annual All-Star game and led the league in scoring in 2006 and 2007. In 2008, he was a member of the U.S. gold medal team at the Beijing Olympics.

On January 22, 2006, Bryant played an unforgettable game against the Toronto Raptors. He had the second highest single game point total in NBA history with 81 points. On that January night, the basketball world realized how well Kobe Bryant could play. Wilt Chamberlain's 100-point game may well be bested by the talented Laker.

EXPERIMENT 4.2

Long Passes Can Be Riskier than Short Passes

MATERIALS
- basketball
- basketball court
- 2 partners
- stopwatch (optional but preferable)
- notebook
- pen or pencil
- calculator (optional)

Players often lose the ball to an opponent by making a long pass. An experiment will show you why such passes can be risky.

1 Stand at one end line on a basketball court. Have a partner with a stopwatch stand on a sideline. If a stopwatch is not available, the partner can count, "One, two, three, four, five," as fast as possible. Each count is very close to $\frac{1}{5}$ of a second. All five equal one second. By such repeated rapid counting, your partner can measure time in seconds and fifths of seconds.

2 Have a second partner stand on the court about 15 feet from you (see Figure 18). Tell the first partner to start the watch or the counting when you release the ball. The watch or counting should be stopped when the second partner catches the ball.

3 Pass the ball to the partner 15 feet from you. How long did it take to complete the pass?

Repeat the experiment several times. What is the average time to complete the pass?

4 See how far you can throw the basketball. Have the partner who catches the ball stand where the ball landed. If you can throw farther than the other end of the court, have him or her stand on the opposite end line from you.

5 Again, tell the first partner to start the watch or the counting when he or she sees you release the ball. The watch or counting should be stopped when the second partner catches the ball.

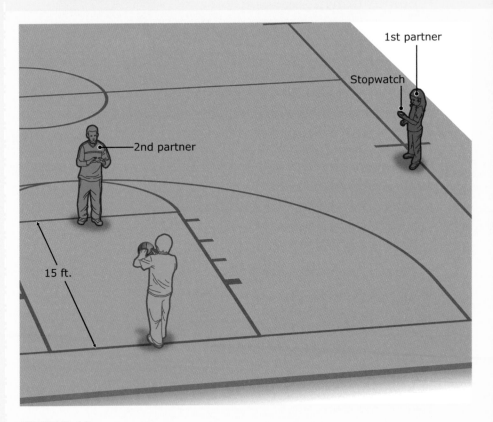

FIGURE 18.
Measure the time it takes to complete passes of different distances.

Repeat the experiment several times. What is the average time to complete the long pass?

How does the time to make a long pass compare with the time to make a shorter pass?

6 Suppose one pass is thrown three times as far as a shorter pass. Does it take three times as long to reach the receiver? Do an experiment to find out.

Why do you think long passes are riskier than short passes?

If passes traveled along straight lines, it would take three times as long for a ball to go three times as far. However, a basketball pass does not travel along straight lines. Gravity constantly pulls the ball downward. To compensate for gravity, the passer gives the ball an upward as well as a horizontal velocity. A short pass that rises only two feet above the point from which it is released will take 0.71 seconds to return to its release height. A long pass that rises 20 feet above the point from which it is released will take 2.24 seconds to return to its release height. Because long passes are in the air longer than short passes, opponents have more time to intercept the ball.

In addition, to increase vertical velocity, the player cannot give the ball as much horizontal velocity. This also increases the time it takes for the ball to reach the receiver.

EXPERIMENT **4.3**

Passes and Vectors

MATERIALS

- ruler
- protractor
- sharp pencil
- notebook or paper, preferably graph paper
- a partner
- basketball
- basketball court

Scientists represent things that have a direction and a size with arrows called vectors. Figure 19a shows some things that can be represented by vectors. The vector's (arrow's) head gives the direction. The vector's length gives the size.

Displacement, which is distance in a particular direction, can be represented by a vector. In Figure 19a, a vector 5.0 cm long represents 10 meters west. The scale for the vector is 1.0 cm = 2.0 m. Another vector 5.0 cm long represents a velocity of 50 mph northeast. The scale for that vector is 1.0 cm = 10 mph. (Remember, a velocity is speed in a certain direction.)

When you pull or push something, you pull or push in a certain direction. Therefore, a force (a push or pull) can be represented by a vector. In Figure 19a, a vector 1 inch long represents a force of 20 newtons south. Each $\frac{1}{4}$ inch represents 5 newtons. The fourth vector represents the acceleration caused by the force of gravity. An acceleration also has a direction as well as size. In this case, the vector is 9.8 cm long. Its scale is 1.0 cm = 1.0 m/s/s. It points down toward Earth's center.

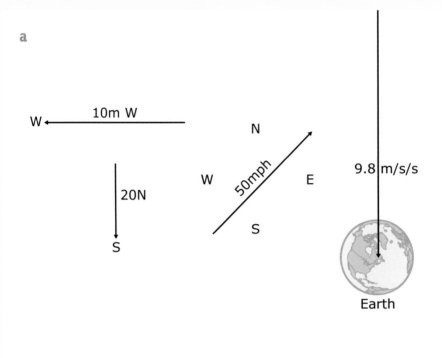

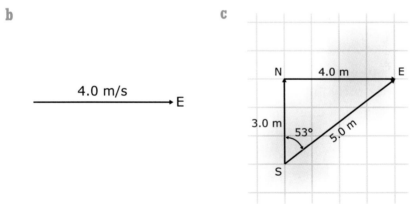

FIGURE 19.

a) These are examples of vectors. They all have direction and size.

b) This vector represents a velocity of 4.0 m/s east.

c) These vectors show the displacement of a teammate who was 3.0 m north of another player, then moved 4.0 m east.

How are vectors related to basketball? Here is an example. You and a teammate are just inside the court's left sideline. You have the ball. Your teammate, who is 3.0 meters (m) in front of you, breaks to the right looking for a pass from you. He or she is running at a speed of 4.0 meters per second (4.0 m/s). At what speed and at what angle should you pass the ball to your teammate?

To answer such a question, you can use vectors. In the case of the teammate, let's say east is to your right. Let 1.0 cm of length represent 1.0 m/s. An arrow 4.0 cm long pointing to the right (east in Figure 19b) can represent your teammate's velocity (4.0 m/s east).

Assume you want your pass to reach your teammate after he or she has traveled 4.0 meters. Since the teammate is running at 4.0 m/s, it will take him or her one second to reach that point. What distance will separate you and your teammate after one second? Vectors provide the answer, and Figure 19c shows you how.

The vector pointing east shows your teammate's position one second after he or she started running. It is 4.0 cm long. The vector pointing north is 3.0 cm long. It shows where your teammate was relative to you before moving. The third vector connects the other two. It shows your teammate's position relative to you after moving 4.0 meters east. That vector is 5.0 cm long and 53 degrees east of north. Since each centimeter represents one meter, your teammate is now 5.0 meters from you at 53 degrees to the right (east of north).

How fast should your pass travel so that he or she catches it at the new position? When should you make the pass?

1 Draw a vector to represent the ball's horizontal velocity. Use a scale of 1.0 cm = 1.0 m/s.

2 Assume you and your teammate are in the same positions as before. This time he or she runs at 4.0 m/s at 45 degrees

east of north. You want your pass to reach your teammate 1.0 second after he or she starts to run. In what direction should your pass travel? How fast should your pass travel?

3 Find a partner and try making similar passes on a basketball court. Learning to make passes that lead (reach the hands of) your moving receiver is as important in basketball as it is in football.

SCIENCE PROJECT IDEA

Use vectors to show how wind can affect basketball shots on an outdoor court. Use vectors to show how players can compensate for the wind when shooting a basketball.

EXPERIMENT **4.4**

The Work to Pass a Basketball

MATERIALS

- basketball
- basketball court
- 2 partners
- stopwatch
- meterstick or yardstick

In science, *work* is carefully defined. Work is the force pulling or pushing something multiplied by the distance the force moves parallel to the moving object. If you push a box 10 meters along the floor with a force of 100 newtons parallel to the motion, you do 1,000 joules of work, because

$$100 \text{ N} \times 10 \text{ m} = 1,000 \text{ J}$$
(1 joule is 1.0 newton x 1.0 meter)

When you lift a basketball, the work you do is the weight of the ball times the height you lift it. The raised ball has potential energy. A basketball, as you know from Experiment 1-1, weighs about 1.3 pounds, or 5.8 newtons. If you lift the ball to a height of 1.0 meter, the work you do is

$$5.8 \text{ N} \times 1.0 \text{ m} = 5.8 \text{ joules}$$

The ball then has 5.8 joules of potential energy. If that ball falls to the floor, it will gain 5.8 joules of kinetic energy just before it hits the floor.

When you throw a basketball, you give it kinetic energy. Its kinetic energy equals the work you do on it. The kinetic energy (KE) of anything is equal to half its mass (m) times its velocity (v) squared:

$$KE = \frac{1}{2} mv^2$$

We know the mass of a basketball is about 0.6 kg. If we measure its velocity, we can find its kinetic energy and the work done on it.

1   Stand at one end line of a basketball court. Have a partner with a stopwatch stand to one side of you. Have a second partner stand on a sideline.

2   Throw the ball with a horizontal velocity. The first partner should start the stopwatch when the ball leaves your hand. He or she should stop the watch when the ball strikes the floor.

3   The second partner should mark the point where the ball lands.

4   Measure the distance the ball traveled.

5   Find the ball's velocity by dividing the distance it traveled by the time on the stopwatch.

For example, if the ball traveled 10 meters in 0.5 second, its velocity was

$$\frac{10 \text{ m}}{0.5 \text{ s}} = 20 \text{ m/s.}$$

Its kinetic energy would be

$$KE = \frac{1}{2} mv^2 = \frac{1}{2} \times 0.6 \text{ kg} \times (20 \text{ m/s})^2 = 120 \text{ J}$$

The work you did on the ball would be 120 joules.

6   With what velocity did you throw the basketball? How much kinetic energy did the ball have? How much work did you do on the ball?

You can also find the average force that you used to throw the ball.

7 Repeat the throw. This time have one partner mark the starting point of your hand just before you throw the ball. Have the second partner mark the point where you release the ball.

8 Use a meterstick or yardstick to measure the distance your hand moved as you threw the ball (1 yard = 0.91 meter).

The average force times the distance your hand moved equals the work you did. You know the work you did equals the ball's kinetic energy.

9 Find the average force you used to throw the ball. For example, if the ball had a kinetic energy of 120 J and your hand moved 2.0 meters, the average force you exerted on the ball would be:

force x distance = 120 J, so force x 2.0 m = 120 J, so force = $\dfrac{120 \text{ J}}{2.0 \text{ m}}$ = 60 N

With how many pounds of force did you throw the ball?

GLOSSARY

acceleration—The rate at which velocity changes.

air pressure—The pressure exerted by air, usually the air in Earth's atmosphere.

angle—A measure of the circle cut off by two straight lines coming from the same point. Angles are measured in degrees.

center of mass (COM)—The point where an object's entire mass can be considered to be located. It is the object's balance point—the point at which forces causing it to rotate are balanced.

circumference—The distance around a circular object.

diameter—The distance across the center of a circular object.

displacement—Distance in a particular direction.

elastic potential energy—The energy stored in a compressed spring, ball, or other object.

first law of motion—An object maintains its state of motion unless acted upon by a force (a push or a pull). An object at rest will remain at rest unless a force acts on it. A moving object will continue to move at the same speed and in the same direction unless a force acts on it.

friction—The force that opposes motion between surfaces that are in contact.

impulse—The force applied to an object multiplied by the time during which the force acts (force × time).

inertia—The property of a stationary object to stay at rest or a moving object to stay in motion.

kinetic energy—The energy of motion. It is equal to $\frac{1}{2}$ the mass of the moving object times the square of its velocity.

mass—The amount of matter in an object. It is measured in kilograms or slugs.

momentum—The mass of an object times its velocity (mass × velocity). It equals the impulse that gave the object its momentum.

potential (gravitational) energy—The energy held by an object that is lifted to a height above the floor. Its potential energy equals the work done in lifting it.

pressure—The force acting on a unit of area.

protractor—An instrument used to measure angles.

second law of motion—An object accelerates when a net force acts on it. Its acceleration is equal to the net force divided by the object's mass.

speed—The distance traveled divided by the time to travel that distance (distance ÷ time).

spring balance—One kind of instrument used to measure forces.

third law of motion—For every action there is an equal and opposite reaction.

vector—An arrow used to represent quantities that have a direction and size, such as displacement, velocity, force, momentum, or acceleration. The vector's (arrow's) head gives the direction. The vector's length gives the size.

velocity—The speed of an object in a particular direction.

weight—The force with which Earth, or any planet, pulls an object toward its center.

work—The net force pulling or pushing something times the distance the force moves parallel to the moving object (force × distance).

FURTHER READING

Bochinski, Julianne Blair. **More Award-Winning Science Fair Projects**. Hoboken, N.J.: John Wiley and Sons, 2004.

Dispezio, Michael A. **Super Sensational Science Fair Projects**. New York: Sterling Publishing, Co., 2002.

Grundy, Pamela, and Susan Shackelford. **Shattering the Glass: The Remarkable History of Women's Basketball**. New York: The New Press, 2005.

Mercer, Bobby. **The Leaping, Sliding, Sprinting, Riding Science Book: 50 Super Sports Science Activities**. New York: Lark Books, 2006.

Levine, Shar & Johnstone, Leslie. **Sports Science**. New York: Sterling Publishing, Co., 2006.

Rhadigan, Joe, and Rain Newcomb. **Prize-Winning Science Fair Projects for Curious Kids**. New York: Lark Books, 2004.

Sudipta, Bardhan-Quallen. **Championship Science Fair Projects: 100 Sure-to-Win Experiments**. New York: Sterling Publishing Co., 2004.

Thomas, Ron. **They Cleared the Lane: The NBA's Black Pioneers**. Lincoln: University of Nebraska Press, 2002.

Thomas, Ron, and Joe Herran. **Getting Into Basketball**. Philadelphia: Chelsea House Publishers, 2006.

Wiese, Jim. **Sports Science: 40 Goal-Scoring, High-Flying, Medal-Winning Experiments for Kids**. New York: John Wiley and Sons, Inc., 2002.

INTERNET ADDRESSES

NBA.
http://www.nba.com

Sport Science: That's the
Way the Ball Bounces.
http://www.exploratorium.
edu/sports/ball_bounces/
index.html

The Basketball and the
Tennis Ball.
http://www.science-projects.
com/Drop/DropBalls.htm

INDEX

ABOUT THE AUTHORS

Robert Gardner is an award-winning author of science books for young people. He is a retired high school teacher of physics, chemistry, and physical science. Dennis Shortelle is a longtime history teacher at Salisbury School in Connecticut. Robert and Dennis have combined to write on a number of diverse topics including Negro League baseball, forensic science, communication, and future studies.